Indian Nations

THE DAKOTA SIOUX

by
Jeanne Oyawin Eder

General Editors
Herman J. Viola and Felix C. Lowe

A Rivilo Book

RAINTREE
STECK-VAUGHN
PUBLISHERS
RSVP ®

A Harcourt Company

Austin · New York
www.steck-vaughn.com

Published by Raintree Steck-Vaughn Company, an imprint of the
Steck-Vaughn Company

Developed for Steck-Vaughn Company by Rivilo Books
Editors: David Jeffery and David Stern   Raintree Steck-Vaughn Publishers Staff
Photo Research: Paula Dailey   Publishing Director: Walter Kossmann
Design: Barbara Lisenby and Todd Hirshman   Editor: Kathy DeVico
Electronic Preparation: Lyda Guz   Electronic Production: Scott Melcer

The photograph of the young boy on the cover was taken in 1984 at a powwow in Cody, Wyoming. He is wearing a headdress made from the hide of a coyote decorated with the feathers of various hawks. Photograph is from the collection of Herman Viola.

Photo Credits: Herman Viola Collection: cover, pp. 11 right, 22, 25; Lisa Ranallo Horse Capture: illustration, pp. 4, 6; Ted Wood: pp. 7, 8, 14, 17, 18 all, 19 top, 20, 27 all, 28, 29, 31 all, 33, 34, 35, 39 all, 40 all, 41 all; National Geographic Image Collection/painting by W. Langdon Kihn: p. 9; Ilka Hartmann: pp. 10, 11 left; National Anthropological Archives, Smithsonian Institution: pp. 12, 15, 19, 23 all, 30, 32, 37, 42; Basgen photography, Minnesota Historical Society: p. 13; National Geographic Image Collection/Thomas Nebbia: p. 16; Nebraska State Historical Society, Lincoln: p. 24 ("Big Missouri's Winter Count"); National Geographic Image Collection/Robert W. Madden: p. 25 left and right (Sioux quillwork by Mrs. Aloysius Newholy); National Geographic Image Collection/Sarah Leen: p. 26.

The editors are grateful to many individuals, families, and organizations for assistance in preparation of this volume. We also wish to thank the Journey Museum, the Sioux Indian Museum in Rapid City, South Dakota, and the National Museum of the American Indian.

Library of Congress Cataloging-in-Publication Data
Eder, Jeanne M. Oyawin.
    The Dakota Sioux/by Jeanne Oyawin Eder.
       p. cm. — (Indian nations)
    Includes bibliographical references and index.
    Summary: Introduces the history, culture, religion, family life,
and tribal government of the Dakota people.
    ISBN 0-8172-5467-6
    1. Dakota Indians — Juvenile literature. [1. Dakota Indians.
2. Indians of North America — Great Plains.] I. Title. II. Series:
Indian nations (Austin, Tex.)
E99.D1E34 2000
978'.0049752—dc21   99-23346
                                            CIP

Printed and bound in the United States
1 2 3 4 5 6 7 8 9 0 LB 03 02 01 00

Contents

White Buffalo Calf Woman

One day long ago, two hunters of the Dakota tribe were out on the Great Plains, searching for the buffalo herds. They spotted something on the distant horizon. As it grew closer, they saw it was a beautiful woman, dressed in white buckskin. On her back she carried a bundle.

The woman said to them: "I am of the Buffalo People. I have been sent to this earth to talk to the Dakota." She commanded them to have a council tipi (tepee) set up in the center of their village, with its door facing east. "I shall be at the village at dawn," she told them.

When the Sun rose in the east, the beautiful woman appeared. From her bundle, she took a pipe stem and a pipe bowl of red stone. Holding the two objects, the beautiful woman addressed everyone. She told them that **Wakan-Tanka**—the Great Spirit—was pleased with the Dakota People. She said that because they had been faithful and had preserved good against evil, the Dakota had been chosen to receive the pipe that she held on behalf of all humankind. Smoking the pipe was to be a bond of good faith between men and nations. A holy man smoking the pipe would be able to send his voice to Wakan-Tanka.

Speaking to the tribe's leader, she explained how to care for the pipe. As **headman**, it was his duty to respect and protect it, since through the pipe the nation lived. As a sacred

◀ *White Buffalo Calf Woman instructed the Dakota to build a council tipi in the center of their village.*

instrument of preservation, the pipe should be used in times of war, famine, sickness, and in other times when the Dakota needed help.

The pipe was also to be used in seven sacred rites the Dakota were to practice: the Rite of Purification, the Keeping of the Soul, Crying for a Vision, the Sun Dance, the Making of Relatives, Preparing a Girl for Womanhood, and the Throwing of the Ball (see pp. 27–29).

Then the beautiful woman left. While walking toward the setting Sun, she stopped and rolled over four times. The first time she became a black buffalo, then a brown buffalo, then a red buffalo. The fourth time she rolled over, she became a white buffalo. Then she disappeared.

This tale is known as the story of White Buffalo Calf Woman. When the Dakota first encountered French traders, they offered to smoke the pipe with them. The French called the Dakota the Indians of the Calumet—a French word for pipe. The pipe became known as the peace pipe.

Creation Story

The Dakota people were nomads. They roamed the woodlands and plains, traveling from place to place in search of the great buffalo herds that lived there. Before the Europeans came to America, buffalo in those herds numbered in the millions.

Buffalo were not just food to the Dakota. As the story of White Buffalo Calf Woman shows, they played a very important part in Dakota legend and religion.

White Buffalo Calf Woman was the goddess Whope, who also appears in the Dakota creation myth. A creation myth is a series of stories that explain how the world came to be. Part of the Dakota creation myth goes like this: Long ago, the god Tate (Wind) lived alone with his four sons, the Four Winds (East, West, North, and South), and his fifth son, little Yumni, the Whirlwind, in their home beyond the pines. Each day, his sons traveled over the world according to Tate's instructions.

One day, when his sons were away, a beautiful woman appeared outside of Tate's tipi. Tate asked her who she was and where she came from. She told him that her name was Whope, that her father was Sun and her mother, Moon, and that she had been sent to the world to find friends.

*At a **powwow**, a modern Dakota girl seems like the goddess Whope reborn.*

When the Four Winds and Whirlwind returned home, they were surprised to find Whope there. That evening, she prepared their favorite meal for each of them. But when their plates remained full no matter how much they ate, they realized that she had supernatural powers. When they discovered that their father thought of Whope not as a wife, but as a daughter, each of the winds wanted her for his partner.

Tipis in a museum stand behind a symbolic map of the sacred four directions of the world.

Soon thereafter, Tate invited all the gods to a feast. He honored his guests with presents. Many told stories of their power, and there was much dancing.

The gods asked Tate how they might please him. He told them that if they honored his daughter, Whope, he himself would be pleased. Then the gods asked Whope what she wanted.

Whope arose and stood by Okaga, the South Wind, who folded his robe around her. "I want a tipi for Okaga and myself, and a place for him and his brothers," she said.

The gods granted her wish. Whope became Okaga's wife. And as a present for the couple and Tate's sons, the gods made them the world and all there is in it.

Prehistory

The Dakota originally lived in and around the upper Mississippi River Valley. The river was central to their way of life. They fished in it for food, built canoes to travel up and down it, and ate the wild rice they found in the marshes surrounding the river.

The Dakota also hunted deer and other game, including buffalo (bison). Some Dakota kept small fields of corn, beans, squash, and sunflowers. They trapped beaver and traded their fur to neighboring tribes for other goods.

When food was scarce in one area, the tribe would move to another. They used dogs to haul their belongings. The dogs were fitted with a sled-type device called a **travois**. A travois was made with two long sticks that were tied across a dog's shoulders. Supplies, bedding, and other equipment were tied onto straps or a net at the other end of the sticks.

For carrying goods from one place to another, the Dakota tied wooden frames called travois to dogs or horses. Then they secured the load to the travois.

The Dakota were constantly at war with many neighboring tribes, including the Chippewa, or Ojibwa tribe, of the Great Lakes region. Around the year 1700, the Ojibwa acquired guns from European settlers, and began forcing the Dakota off their native lands and westward onto the Great Plains.

At this time, the Dakota nation split into three main divisions. The Western, or Teton, Division was the largest and most powerful. They lived in North Dakota and South Dakota. The Middle Division did not have a separate name. They lived in parts of North Dakota. The Eastern, or Santee Division, lived mostly in Minnesota.

For many years, the Dakota were known as the Sioux Indians. The name Sioux came from the Ojibwa, who called the Dakota the *Nadessioux*, which means "enemies." Early French explorers shortened this to Sioux.

Scholars now classify all the Dakota people of the plains as belonging to the Siouan language family. Other tribes that belong to this large language family are the Mandan, Hidatsa, Crow, Iowa, Oto, Missouri, Omaha, Ponca, Osage, and Kansa.

The three divisions of the Dakota Nation prefer to be called either "Lakota" (Teton Division), "Nakota" (Middle Division), or the "Dakota" (Santee Division). All those names are translated as "friends."

A barrette to hold hair in place names the three divisions of the Dakota—all meaning "friends."

Key Historical Events

Encounters with the French

Even in their early Minnesota home, the Dakota were expert traders. From nearby tribes they acquired seashells to decorate their clothing and special stones like flint to use as tools and weapons. In return they traded decorated buffalo hides, dried buffalo meat called **jerky**, and clothing decorated with dyed porcupine quills.

In 1640 the Dakota met their first Europeans, a group of French explorers. French traders soon followed. These men wanted the furs of animals that lived in Dakota country. In exchange, they introduced the Dakota to goods such as flint and steel "strike-a-lights." When struck together, these strike-a-lights produced sparks to light a fire. These traders also brought glass beads, metal knives and axes, guns, flour, sugar, and coffee to the Dakota.

Dentalium shells strung with fine workmanship give brilliance to the shawl of a young woman (right).
A woman adjusts the shell-and-stone decorated dress for her granddaughter's first dance at a powwow (below).

The Louisiana Purchase

At first the Dakota were able to enjoy the benefits brought to them by the traders. They did not suffer much upset to their way of life, because few white people lived in their country. Then, in 1804, the United States made the Louisiana Purchase, buying from France most of the land extending from the Mississippi River to the Rocky Mountains and the Gulf of Mexico to Canada.

The U.S. government sent explorers Meriwether Lewis and William Clark to explore the newly purchased territory. During the two-year expedition, Lewis and Clark crossed Dakota territory and met with members of several bands. Within a few decades, thousands of white settlers followed the path blazed by Lewis and Clark.

With the white man came disease. **Smallpox** killed thousands of Dakota people in 1818, 1845, and 1850. When gold was discovered in California in 1849, prospectors by the thousands headed west to seek their fortunes. To get to the California goldfields, many of the miners passed through Dakota country. This greatly upset the Dakota, who protested that the miners seemed to care nothing for the rights of others, especially Indians.

In 1851 the U.S. government and the Dakota signed the first in a series of treaties at Fort Laramie, in what is now Wyoming. In the Fort Laramie Treaty, the Dakota promised that white people could pass safely through their lands as long as they stayed on specified routes, such as the Oregon and Bozeman trails.

Government officials meet with Dakota leaders in 1868 to sign the final treaty at Fort Laramie. The Indians are, from left: Packs His Drum, Old Man Afraid of His Horses, and Red Bear.

But few of the thousands of cross-country travelers honored the Fort Laramie Treaty. Some walked, some rode horses, but most traveled in large trains of covered wagons. With them were thousands of cows, horses, and mules that ate the grass, leaving less for the buffalo, antelope, and deer, which the Indians hunted. To make matters worse, instead of enforcing the Fort Laramie Treaty, the government pressured the tribe to make more land available to white settlers.

The Great Sioux Uprising

The thousands of white people who came west seeking their land frightened and angered the Dakota. The buffalo were disappearing, and the Dakota way of life was being threatened. Beginning in 1855 tensions between the Dakota and their white neighbors increased until, in 1862, they erupted into a full-scale war known as the Great Sioux Uprising.

The cause of the uprising was the failure of the U.S. government to honor agreements it had made with Dakota bands living in Minnesota. These people had sold much of their traditional homelands to make room for more settlers to live. The U.S. government, however, had failed to make the payments of money and food promised in the treaties.

At the Fort Snelling Stockade, peaceful Dakota camp while awaiting their fate after the Great Sioux Uprising. They were resettled in Nebraska.

In fairness, the United States was preoccupied with fighting the Civil War. But excuses such as this one did not put food in the mouths of the starving Dakota women and children. Angry at the government for not keeping its promises, the Dakota attacked and killed hundreds of white settlers.

The U.S. government retaliated by sending in the army. In the brutal war that followed, hundreds of Dakota were killed, and the survivors were forced to leave Minnesota entirely.

The Battle of the Little Bighorn

In an effort to bring an end to these conflicts, the United States government established the Great Sioux Reservation in 1868. The reservation was a huge tract of land that included most of present-day North and South Dakota. It was set aside, or "reserved," for the Dakota. The Indians who already lived on reservation land were expected to learn the ways of white people and to stop roaming the plains. Those who lived outside the reservations were expected to move to them. All Dakota were to become farmers, speak English, and practice white people's religions.

In the southwestern corner of the Great Sioux Reservation, there was an area known as the Black Hills. These hills were sacred to the Dakota, who called them "Paha Sapa." Many religious and ceremonial sites were within the Black Hills. The Black Hills also contained the most fertile soil on the entire reservation. The Dakota spent

The Paha Sapa range in the Black Hills was sacred to the Dakota. When gold was found nearby in 1874, white people rushed to mine it.

much of their summers there, gathering berries that grew so abundantly and in the dense forests cutting poles for their tipis.

But in 1874 an expedition led by Lieutenant Colonel George Armstrong Custer discovered gold in the Black Hills. As soon as this news became public, white people rushed there, ignoring the Ft. Laramie Treaty. Rather than force the gold miners to leave, the United States tried to buy the Black Hills from the tribe. The Dakota refused to sell.

Meanwhile, several bands of the Dakota refused to move onto the Great Sioux Reservation. These bands were led by great warriors such as Crazy Horse and Gall, and wise men such as Sitting Bull. These strong-willed leaders had never signed any treaties and wanted to remain free to hunt and to travel where they wished.

Angry at the Dakota because of the Black Hills issue, the U.S. government ordered all the Dakota to move onto the Great Sioux Reservation during the winter of 1875. Those who did not would be considered hostile and be attacked or punished.

The winter was particularly harsh that year. Even if they had tried, the bands would not have been able to move to the distant reservation by the deadline. Some bands never even received news of the deadline. Nonetheless, U.S. Army troops began attacking the various bands of Dakota found off the reservation. Many men, women, and children were killed.

Sitting Bull, Dakota spiritual leader, said that by defeating Lieutenant Colonel Custer and his U.S. soldiers: "We have won a great battle but lost a great war."

Indian horsemen ride up "Custer Hill" during a reenactment of the famous fight at Little Bighorn Battlefield National Monument in eastern Montana.

Rather than surrender, however, the independent Dakota bands joined together with Cheyenne and Arapaho allies into one large village under the leadership of Sitting Bull. On June 25, 1876, Custer surprised the village at its camp along the banks of the Little Bighorn River in present-day southeastern Montana. Custer and more than 200 of his soldiers were killed in what is now known as the Battle of the Little Bighorn.

Sitting Bull, Crazy Horse, and Gall won a great victory, but the Dakota were soon defeated by other armies. Within a year, all the Indians who had fought Custer were either dead, living on reservations, or had escaped to Canada.

In revenge for the Battle of the Little Bighorn, the U.S. government demanded that the Dakota give up the Black Hills. By now, buffalo were nearly extinct, and the Indians depended on the government for their food. Having no other choice, the chiefs signed over the Black Hills to the United States government in 1877. The treaty they signed also called for all the Dakota to live on reservations.

Bison, called buffalo, graze in the Black Hills. Sacred to the Dakota, buffalo were shot almost to extinction.

The Ghost Dance and the Battle of Wounded Knee

In 1890 a **shaman** named Wovoka from the Paiute tribe claimed to have had a vision where he saw God and all the people who had died a long time ago. He called on Indians everywhere to perform the Ghost Dance. The Ghost Dance, he claimed, would bring back the buffalo and cause the white man to disappear. Dead Indians would also return to Earth.

For the Dakota, that summer of 1890 on their reservations was a disaster. The crops the white man insisted that they grow failed; starvation seemed certain. They saw in the Ghost Dance a chance to return to their old way of life.

Nearby white settlers and army leaders saw danger. When Sitting Bull proclaimed himself a believer in the Ghost Dance, the army decided to arrest him. The chief, now an old man, would not go peacefully, and was shot dead on December 14, 1890, by reservation police who claimed that he was "attempting to resist arrest."

The final tragedy for the Dakota nation came two weeks later. Led by Chief Big Foot, who was dying of pneumonia, 153 members of his Miniconjou Dakota band, who had been

Dakota horsemen ride in bitter cold to observe the 100th anniversary of the slaughter at the "battle" of Wounded Knee. This marker (left) is a memorial to those who died there.

trying to hide from the U.S. Army, surrendered in bitter cold weather to the 7th Cavalry at Wounded Knee Creek in South Dakota. A small scuffle broke out between the warriors and the troopers. Suddenly from close range, the soldiers fired repeating cannons at the Dakota, killing 144 of them. Among the dead were 44 women and 18 children.

Although this encounter has been called the Battle of Wounded Knee, it was really a massacre, or slaughter. It was also the last armed conflict between the Dakota and the U.S. government. Wounded Knee ended active Dakota resistance.

Way of Life

The Dakota's entire way of life changed when they moved to the Great Plains. The buffalo became essential to their existence. Buffalo meat was not only cooked, but dried to make jerky. Pemmican, a healthy snack eaten while traveling, was a mixture of ground up dried meat, fresh berries, and buffalo fat.

Buffalo provided hides for beds, moccasins, and clothing. Buffalo hide could also be used for bow cases, gun covers, knife sheaths, **quivers**, shields, rope, and many other useful products. Parfleches—boxes used for storing food and household items—were made from rawhide (untanned buffalo skin). Buffalo hooves were made into glue, hoes, and axes, and other tools were made from buffalo bones. **Sinew** was used for bow strings as well as for sewing thread. Buffalo horns were made

Parfleches, or boxes for storing food and tools, were sometimes highly decorated (left). They were made by stretching buffalo hide with pegs (below) and laying out designs on the hide.

into ladles and spoons. The buffalo's stomach became a large cooking pot for stews. The bladder became a water container. The tail became a fly swatter. In fact, just about every part of the buffalo was useful for something. Even its manure, called "buffalo chips," provided the fuel used in campfires.

Originally, the Dakota hunted buffalo by driving them over cliffs. The buffalo would be badly hurt or killed in the fall. But by the end of the 1700s, horses had transformed the lives of the Plains tribes. Dakota hunters could gallop alongside running buffalo and shoot them with a bow and arrow.

The gun made it even easier to hunt buffalo. It also helped make the numerous and militant Dakota the most fearsome warriors on the plains.

Food

The Dakota diet was nutritious and tasty. Soups and stews were made with roots and berries and meat from wild game, such as buffalo, antelope, deer, and elk. These stews were cooked by a method called stone boiling. Food was placed into a container of water—usually a hole in the ground lined with

Stews made from roots, berries, and meat are still cooked by boiling, and the pot is stirred with deer horn.

the stomach of a buffalo. Hot stones were then put in the water. As those stones cooled, they were removed and replaced with new, hotter ones. In minutes, the water would come to a boil and cook the food.

Large pieces of meat were cooked in a different way. A cooking pit was dug and filled with red hot coals. The meat was placed on top of the coals and covered with grass or leaves. Then everything was buried under a layer of dirt, creating a simple but efficient oven.

Nature also provided plants and herbs that the Dakota used to treat ailments and injuries. Here are a few of the medicines from nature's chest and what they were used for:

inner willow bark	fevers
cedar	coughs
cattails	burns
wild rose	eye inflammation
wild plum	skin scrapes
wild licorice	toothache
milkweed	stomach troubles
horsemint	stomach pain
wild mint	**colic**
ragweed	nausea, headaches

Houses

The Dakota lived in tents they called tipis. The tipi was a tall, cone-shaped structure made of flexible, tanned buffalo hides. A small one used seven buffalo hides. A large tipi used 12 to 18 hides. An average tipi measured 11 feet (3.4 m) across at its base. It was held up by long, slender poles made from the trunks of young pine trees.

Tipis were comfortable to live in. The furniture inside consisted of painted backrests. They were used like recliner chairs and made out of willow branches. Each tipi also contained a fire pit and a sleeping area.

Women built the tipis and were considered their owners. They were responsible for putting up the tipi and taking it down. This is why the Dakota gave all the parts of their tipi feminine names.

Among the most unusual tipis were ones made by children of the victorious bands following the Battle of the Little Bighorn. They made their miniature tipis with paper money taken from dead soldiers.

Today the Dakota people live in houses, but they still use tipis for ceremonies and camping out at powwows. Powwows are social gatherings where Indian families come together to dance, sing, and enjoy one another's friendship.

A hide tipi is decorated with a buffalo tail, and buffalo ears become pockets for tent poles.

Clothing

The Dakota made their winter clothing from tanned buffalo hides: pants and shirts for the men, dresses for the women. Both men and women also wore robes made from buffalo hides with the hair still on them.

On nice summer days, men usually wore simple breechcloths—a long strip of leather that passed between the legs and hung front and back from a strap around the waist. Women, however, always wore dresses.

Both men and women wore moccasins, but women's moccasins often had high tops to protect their legs from thorns and thistles while they collected berries and plants.

The war shirt of Kicking Bird (right) seen close-up (above) reveals fringe, finely beaded panels, and locks of human hair, most likely from his relatives.

Arts and Crafts

The art of the Dakota is both useful and beautiful to look at. "Winter Counts" are an important Dakota art form. Winter Counts are pictures painted on animal hides of important events in tribal life. The Dakota used these pictures to tell their history.

One picture was usually drawn each year. An older member of the tribe, known as Keeper of the Winter Count, was responsible for drawing the picture and remembering what it represented. The Keeper recorded events such as battles with neighboring tribes, sicknesses, and the arrival of strangers in their land.

Each year, the Keeper of the Winter Count added one picture of the year's most important event to a large hide. The one shown below is from about 1926.

The Dakota people decorated their clothes with porcupine quills. Women made beautiful and elaborate ceremonial outfits. Everyday objects, such as a baby's **cradleboard** and storage boxes, were also decorated.

After being plucked from a porcupine's **carcass**, the quills were cleaned and dyed different colors. The dye colors came from soaking the quills in water that contained fruits, grasses, or clays of different colors. Some Dakota still use quills to decorate things they make.

Early settlers introduced glass beads to the Dakota people. Since beads were easier to use than porcupine quills, most women preferred them for decorating their clothes. The beads were embroidered onto dresses, shirts, and moccasins in geometric patterns, which are still popular Dakota art designs.

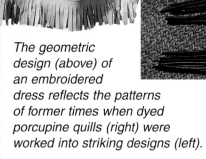

The geometric design (above) of an embroidered dress reflects the patterns of former times when dyed porcupine quills (right) were worked into striking designs (left).

Spiritual Life

Dakota people believe that there is one supreme being. His name is Wakan-Tanka. His power and energy is in all living things. The Dakota call this spiritual force **Wakan** (Wah-KON) and believe it can be found everywhere. Rocks, animals, trees, even the winds and the rains have Wakan.

Living on the plains, the Dakota were dependent on nature for their existence. They gave names to the most powerful forces of nature and prayed to them for good fortune in their daily lives. These forces were also considered gods, who were all part of Wakan-Tanka.

Chief among them was the Sun—Wi (WEE). He was the defender of bravery, fortitude (strength of mind), generosity, and fidelity (loyalty). Skan—Sky—was the judge of all gods and spirits. Earth—Maka—was the mother of all the spirits and all living things that grew from the earth. Inyan—Rock—was the ancestor of all gods and all things; he was also patron of construction.

Other gods included Tate, or the Wind, who governed the seasons, and Hanwi, or the Moon, the wife of the Sun, who set the time for all important events. Tatanka, the Buffalo God, determined the success or failure of the buffalo hunt. Whope, the daughter of the Sun and Moon (also known as the Beautiful One) was the Great Mediator and patron of harmony and pleasure.

Only once in a million times—or more— does a buffalo give birth to a white calf. It is held to be sacred by the Dakota.

26

The Seven Sacred Rites

When she came to Earth as White Buffalo Calf Woman, Whope brought the Dakota the sacred pipe. This pipe was used in the seven rites that enabled the Dakota to communicate with Wakan-Tanka. The seven rites were: The Rite of Purification, The Keeping of the Soul, Crying for a Vision, The Sun Dance, The Making of Relatives, Preparing a Girl for Womanhood, and The Throwing of the Ball.

The Rite of Purification had to be performed before any of the other rites could take place. This rite consisted of going into a sweat lodge and sweating out the impurities of the body and of the mind.

The sweat lodge was made from willows bent to form a low, dome-shaped structure. The dome was covered with hides, and a hole was dug in the center. A fire pit was built outside the sweat lodge. Rocks were placed into this fire.

Children gather fragrant sage to be used in the purifying ceremony (above). A spiritual leader arranges sage bundles on the floor of a sweat house under construction (left).

A man shovels fire-heated rocks into the sweat lodge. When water is poured on the rocks, steam rises, and the people inside are cleansed in body and spirit.

When the rocks were heated to a glowing red, they were put into the hole inside the sweat lodge.

Water was then splashed on the hot rocks, producing steam. Those inside the lodge offered prayers while they sweated. Everyone emerged from the sweat lodge refreshed and renewed. The sweat lodge is similar to the sauna widely used today.

The Vision Quest was used to prepare for battle, to ask for a divine favor, or, more generally, to pray for guidance. A seeker of the vision, usually, though not always, a man, goes to a holy man who prays for him. After time spent in the sweat lodge, the seeker goes into the wilderness. There he stays for days without food, praying for a vision to understand his relation to all things and to gain knowledge of the Great Spirit. The vision often comes to the seeker as a dream in the form of an animal or of an element of nature. Finally, friends bring the seeker back to the village, where the holy man listens to the seeker's vision and interprets its meaning.

The Sun Dance was the most important of all the rites to the Dakota people. It was held during the summer under the full moon of June or July, a time when the entire Dakota nation gathered together to feast and celebrate. The Sun Dance was performed so that men could worship and ask favors of Wi, the

Sun God. A special sun lodge, usually a large tipi, was erected. Into it was brought the trunk of a cottonwood tree, which represented a conquered enemy. It was set into the ground. A sweat lodge was built around the tree trunk. Dancers entered the lodge and purified themselves. Each then pierced his flesh and had rawhide thongs threaded through the wounds and tied to the tree. The men danced until the thongs broke free. The tearing of the flesh represented freeing the body from ignorance. After the ceremonies a feast was held.

The U.S. government considered these sacrifices, especially piercing the skin, a form of self-torture, so it outlawed the Sun Dance in 1883. In modern times, however, the Sun Dance has been revived as an important spiritual journey in a Dakota's life.

A Dakota man sets out sacred buffalo skulls on the grounds where the traditional Sun Dance will be held.

Family Life

Clans

Among the Dakota, people related by blood or marriage lived together as a group called a **tiyospaye** (tee-yo-SPAH-yay). Children belonging to the same tiyospaye played together. The men hunted together, and the women cooked together.

In this system everyone had lots of family. Everyone had a mother and father, and brothers and sisters. There were no children without parents and no parents without children. Orphans were absorbed into their extended family, usually raised by grandparents or aunts. When you came into the world as a baby, you were surrounded by a loving family. When you died, you were surrounded by a loving family.

Sitting Bull's family portrait included his mother, Her-Holy-Door, and his eldest daughter, Many Horses, who holds her son, name unknown.

At a ceremony, four generations of a family honor one another and those who served in the U.S. Armed Forces.

Even today, the most important thing for each of the Dakota people is to be a good relative. Be a good brother or a good sister! Be a good mother or father! Having close blood relatives helped the Dakota people struggle united together through their hardest times, when intertribal fighting and diseases killed so many.

A mother helps prepare her daughter for a dance.

Women and Children

The main role of women was to keep the household. They prepared the meat after the hunt and made the clothing the family wore. Women raised the children and taught the young girls the skills they would need when they married.

Children were allowed to play and be carefree until they were old enough to help with chores, such as collecting firewood and hauling water. When children began to reach maturity, they were expected to contribute to the tribe by learning to hunt and to take care of the household.

Warriors

Though men spent much of their time hunting, their primary role in the tribe was as warriors. Warrior societies governed the tribe and protected women, children, and the elderly from tribal enemies such as the Arikara, the Blackfoot, and the Crow.

Warfare was a necessity to the Dakota not only for defense, but also to provide opportunities for young men to gain the honor and prestige necessary for leadership. Warfare among the Plains tribes was more like a sport than mortal combat. The highest honor was achieved not by killing the enemy but by "counting coup" upon the enemy. Counting coup meant hitting an enemy without necessarily killing him. It was an act of bravery and daring that brought much prestige. For the victim, however, it meant dishonor.

One of 41 color-pencil drawings by Red Horse, who was at Little Bighorn, shows warriors leading away prized U.S. cavalry horses.

Another part of war was the taking of scalps from enemies who died in battle. Scalps were taken as a sign of victory. They were also a symbol of honor that the Dakota sometimes used as decoration on their shirts or horse gear.

Warriors desired to be noted for their bravery and generosity. One of the bravest deeds was to sneak into an enemy village, capture a prized horse, and then give it to a poor Dakota woman who had no horses.

Games

Many Dakota games were designed to prepare children for adulthood. Boys hunted small animals like rabbits, gophers, and prairie dogs. Girls created little villages and put up miniature tipis.

The Dakota especially enjoyed athletic games like foot racing, horse racing, and target shooting. These games helped boys build up their physical strength and taught them the skills needed to be successful hunters and warriors. For example, in the game known as "Hoop and Pole," boys threw little spears called darts at a hoop rolling across the grass. The object of the game was to throw the dart through the rolling hoop without knocking it over. The game helped boys gain the skills necessary for hitting a running animal with a spear.

An athletic game played by children and adults alike was "Shinny." It was a team sport played on a large field with goals at either end. Players carried shinny sticks, which they used to hit or to carry a small ball across the field to the goal. The game was comparable to today's lacrosse or field hockey.

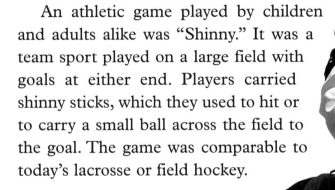

Of many games and sports, none was better loved by the Dakota than racing horses.

Tribal Government

The Dakota did not have a full-time tribal government. Only when the tribes assembled for the Sun Dance were questions of policy discussed. For the rest of the year, the tribes or bands operated independently.

The Dakota always tried to organize by the sacred numbers of four and seven. The largest group of the nation was called the Seven Council Fires. Within this group there were camps at each of the four cardinal directions: north, east, west, and south. Each camp could consist of seven bands. Each of these bands was usually named after its leader. Within each band there were four families.

Each family had a headman. Although a headman's son could inherit his father's position in the band, this was not guaranteed. Whoever hoped to be chief had to prove himself to be a successful hunter and a good warrior. He also had to demonstrate a generous heart by giving horses, food, and other valuable presents to friends, relatives, and the needy.

Within each tribe there were also several societies that served civil or police functions. The Buffalo Headdress Society was responsible for watching over the entire village. Members of the White Horse Owners Society had reputations as good hunters.

An entrance sign at the Pine Ridge Reservation honors famous past chiefs and spiritual leaders Red Cloud, Black Elk, and Crazy Horse.

Each society had its own name and a special place or tipi in which to hold ceremonies. Some societies had their own designs or clothes, much as uniforms today identify the wearer as a boy scout, nurse, police officer, or soldier. The two most important societies were the Akicita, or tribal police, and the warriors.

When the Dakota were forced onto reservations, the U.S. government's **Bureau of Indian Affairs** took charge of all the tribes' matters, including those formerly controlled by the societies. Because the Bureau would deal only with the chiefs of each tribe, the societies lost their importance and disappeared.

Today each of the Dakota tribes is governed by a tribal council elected by its members. Tribal members age 18 years or older may vote.

At Pine Ridge, grazing land ends with the rocky rise of what are called "badlands."

Contemporary Life

Dakota reservations are located in several states. In Nebraska there is the Santee Reservation. In South Dakota there are the Rosebud, Standing Rock, Yankton, Pine Ridge, Lower Brule, Crow Creek, Cheyenne River, and Sisseton-Wahpeton reservations. In North Dakota there are the Standing Rock and Spirit Lake reservations. In Montana there is the Fort Peck Reservation, inhabited by the Assiniboine and the Sioux.

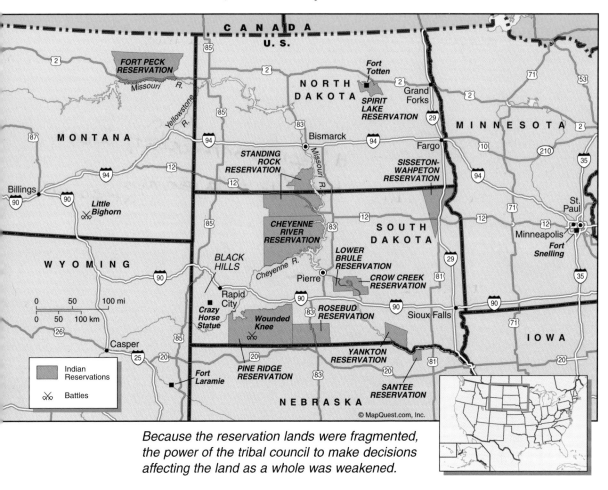

Because the reservation lands were fragmented, the power of the tribal council to make decisions affecting the land as a whole was weakened.

The years following their confinement to reservations were hard ones for the Dakota. The land was not suited to farming, and the Dakota people were not suited to the regimented lifestyle of farmers.

Another problem was that much of the original Dakota reservation lands had been illegally sold to white settlers. Even before the final boundaries of the reservations had been established, nine million acres were sold to white settlers. This resulted in a "checkerboard-style" settlement of the land, with the boundaries between Indian and white territory unclear. Because authority over individual plots of land was fragmented by this checkerboard-style settlement, the power of the tribal council was greatly weakened in deciding issues that affected the reservation lands as a whole.

The Indian Reorganization Act of 1934 was a major turning point in relations between Native Americans everywhere and the U.S. government. This act established the concept of political self-determination for the tribes, and provided the Dakota with an annual $2-million fund to purchase new tribal lands.

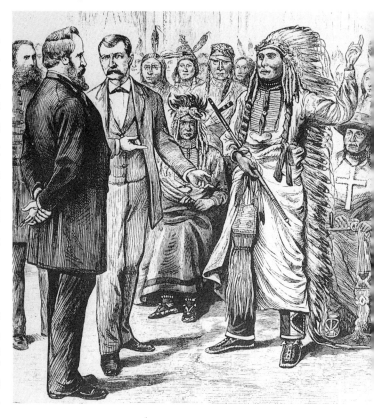

When Spotted Tail, Red Cloud, and others visited President Hayes in 1877, he told them that the "white people [were] a great multitude" who would sweep over them unless they settled and began to farm.

Conflicts with the United States

The armed struggle between the United States government and the Dakota had ended long ago, but the two governments still clashed. In 1942 the United States seized 500 square miles (1,300 sq km) of the Sioux Pine Ridge Reservation to use as a practice bombing range.

In 1943 the Missouri River flooded. It caused great damage and loss of life along its banks downstream from Dakota country. Despite protests made by the Dakota, the U.S. government decided to dam the river upstream, to prevent such disasters from occurring again. The Pick-Sloan program created more than one hundred dams and flooded more than 202,000 acres (81,750 ha) of Dakota land. As a result, hundreds of Dakota families were forced to move. Homes, crops, pasture, and their most valuable timberland were flooded. Churches, community centers, cemeteries, and shrines had to be moved. This action by the United States government destroyed the Indians' economic base for the second time in less than a century.

One dispute the Dakota have never stopped arguing about is the return of the Black Hills. In 1887 the old chiefs formed an organization in protest of the takeover. However, it was not until 1923 that the Dakota filed a claim formally requesting the return of the Black Hills from the United States. Then, after 57 more years of fighting in U.S. courtrooms, the Dakota people finally received justice. On June 30, 1980, the Supreme Court of the United States agreed that the Black Hills had been taken away illegally from the Dakota people. Even though the Supreme Court refused to return the Black Hills to the Dakota, it awarded the tribe a substantial amount of money for the loss of the land.

The Future

Most Dakota families today have televisions, telephones, and may have computers. Every reservation has communities with stores, churches, schools, coffee shops, office buildings, hospitals, and some museums. There are also many individually owned farms and ranches.

But the adjustment to the white man's world is not complete. Recent statistics show that tribal members on the Pine Ridge Reservation die younger than any other group in the nation. There is also widespread poverty, and continual health problems, such as diabetes and alcoholism on the reservations.

But despite hard times, the Dakota people have managed to preserve many of their traditional values and religious beliefs. They continue with the Sun Dances, the sweat lodge ceremonies, and their old

Dakota children are in some ways like modern kids everywhere. But they are also taught their traditions, such as drumming and singing (right) and learning by imitation how to dance (below).

songs. The young people today are taught about the White Buffalo Calf Woman and her seven sacred rites.

The Dakota are proud of their love of nature and their warrior heritage. They also take pride in the many places across the United States that carry Dakota names, such as North and South Dakota; Red Cloud, Nebraska; and Santee, Nebraska.

In the Black Hills of South Dakota, a huge statue of Crazy Horse is being blasted out of a mountain. It will be the largest sculpture in the world, measuring 563 feet (172 m) high and

An enormous copy of a small statue of Crazy Horse (inset) is being blasted from a mountain in South Dakota.

641 feet (195 m) long. After Mt. Rushmore, it is one of the most popular sights in South Dakota. People all over the world already come to see it. They find inspiration in the size of the project and the heroic representation of Crazy Horse, the great warrior who was never photographed in his own lifetime.

The Dakota today are college graduates, businesspeople, homemakers, factory workers, and art and museum curators. They live a modern life while staying true to their old traditions and are proud to be both Dakota Indian and American.

A spiritual leader honors veterans in a sacred pipe ceremony (above). Eagle feather fans, face paint, and an American flag adorn a veteran who honors two nations (left).

Dakota Sioux Activity

The Dakota used Winter Counts as a "written" account of their history. You can make a Winter Count that shows your own personal history. You will need a large brown paper bag, color markers, and your imagination!

Cut the paper bag so it will lay flat. Then crumple the paper together until it feels soft and pliable in your hands. Be careful not to over-soften it so that it gets holes in it. When the entire bag is softened, it should look and feel somewhat like a piece of leather. Cut, or better, carefully tear, the sides to make the bag take the shape of a real buffalo hide.

Once you have your "hide" made, use your markers to write your history. Start with the year you were born. In the middle of your hide, draw a picture of the most important thing that happened that year. From there, go around in a spiral, ever outward, drawing a picture (one for every year) of the events that were most significant to you.

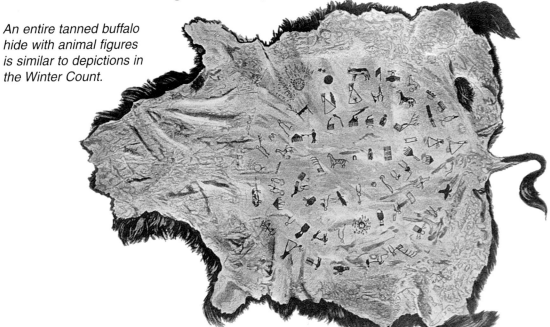

An entire tanned buffalo hide with animal figures is similar to depictions in the Winter Count.

Dakota Sioux Song

Dakota people respected all plants and animals, and they had special songs for many of them. Here is the song a Dakota woman would sing when collecting wild roses:

From the heart of the mother we come,

The kind mother of life and of all;

And if ever you think she is dumb,

You should know that flowers are her songs.

And all creatures that live are her songs,

And all creatures that die are her songs.

And the winds blowing by are her songs,

And she wants you to sing all her songs.

Like the purple in Daydawn we come,

And our hearts are so brimful of joy

That whene'er we're not singing we hum

Ti-li-li-li-i, ta-la-la-loo, ta-la-la-loo!

Dakota Sioux Recipe

On special occasions, the Dakota people would often make a dessert treat called wojapi (WO-zha-pee). It is also called berry pudding. They ate it either by itself or with bread.

To make wojapi, you need:

1 small bag of frozen berries (blueberries work well)
1 cup sugar
1/2 cup flour

Directions:

Thaw the berries, and add them to a cup of water in a saucepan. Add the flour and then the sugar, stirring carefully. Continue to stir over medium heat, until the mixture thickens. Then it is ready to serve.

Dakota Sioux Prayer

The light of Wakan-Tanka is upon my people:

It is making the whole earth bright.

My people are now happy!

All beings that move are rejoicing!

Further Reading

Bunting, Eve. *Moonstick: The Seasons of the Sioux*. New York: Harpercollins, 1997.

Eastman, Charles A. *Wigwam Evenings, Sioux Folk Tales Retold*. Lincoln, Nebraska: University of Nebraska Press, 1990.

McGinnis, Mark W. *Lakota & Dakota Animal Wisdom Stories*. Chamberlain, SD: St. Joseph's Indian School: Tipi Press, 1994.

Mclaughlin, Marie. *Myths and Legends of the Sioux*. Lincoln, Nebraska: University of Nebraska Press, 1990.

Sources

Brown, Joseph Epes (recorded and edited by). *The Sacred Pipe: Black Elk's Account of the Seven Rites of the Oglala Sioux*. Norman, OK: University of Oklahoma Press, 1953.

Standing Bear, Luther. *My People, The Sioux*. Boston: Houghton Mifflin, 1928.

Utley, Robert M. *The Last Days of the Sioux Nation*. New Haven: Yale University Press, 1963.

Viola, Herman J. *North American Indians: An Introduction to the Lives of America's Native Peoples, from the Inuit of the Arctic to the Zuni of the Southwest*. New York: Crown Publishers, 1996.

Viola, Herman J. *Little Bighorn Remembered: The Untold Indian Story of Custer's Last Stand*. New York: Times Books, 1999.

Dakota Sioux Chronology

1600s	The Dakota move onto the Great Plains.
1640	The first written mention of the Dakota is recorded by French explorers.
1700s	Horses and guns are introduced.
1804	Lewis & Clark meet the Dakota Sioux.
1842	The Oregon Trail is established; the first wagons cross Dakota's Territory.
1849	California gold rush
1851	The Fort Laramie Treaty recognizes Sioux ownership of 60 million acres of land.
1862	"Great Sioux Uprising:" Minnesota (Santee) Dakota declare war on white settlers.
1868	The "Great Sioux Reservation" is established.
1874	Gold is discovered in the Black Hills of South Dakota.
1876	Battle of the Little Bighorn
1889	The Great Sioux Reservation is broken up into six separate reservations.
1890	Death of Sitting Bull Wounded Knee Massacre
1934	The Indian Reorganization Act is passed. It reverses the decades-old policy of forcing Indians to adopt white ways and provides for increased tribal sovereignty.
1943	The Pick-Sloan Program is passed; reservation lands are flooded.
1973	American Indian Movement (A.I.M.) occupies town of Wounded Knee at gunpoint to protest for Indian rights.
1980	The U.S. Supreme Court awards the Dakota $106 million for the unlawful taking of the Black Hills.
1991	A Century of Reconciliation is declared between South Dakota and Nine Tribal Governments.

Glossary

Bureau of Indian Affairs The agency that carries out U. S. government laws, treaties, and policies related to American Indians.

Carcass The remains of a dead animal.

Colic Minor abdominal pain.

Cradleboard Traditional child-rearing papoose used to protect and carry babies and infants.

Headman The leader of the Dakota Sioux tribe.

Jerky Dried meat.

Powwow An Indian cultural gathering and celebration. Dancers and singers perform and pay tribute to one another, family members, veterans, and other community leaders.

Quiver A tube or case used for holding arrows.

Shaman A holy person with powers to cure illness.

Sinew Animal tendon treated to act as a cord.

Smallpox A disease that is easily spread and often deadly. It is caused by a virus. A person with smallpox has a high fever and puss-filled bumps on the skin that can leave deep, permanent scars.

Tiyospaye A kinship term for a family division of the tribe.

Travois A sled-type device. It is made with two long sticks tapered to one end and connected with straps or a net at the other.

Wakan Having the characteristic of being sacred or being spiritual.

Wakan-Tanka The creator of all things; the Great Spirit.

Index

Numbers in italics indicate illustration or map.

MAR - 2002

Pub